Key Facts™ on

Bahrain

~Essential Information on Bahrain~

By Patrick W. Nee

The Internationalist®

www.internationalist.com

The Internationalist®

International Business, Investment, and Travel

Published by:

The Internationalist Publishing Company

96 Walter Street/ Suite 200

Boston, MA 02131, USA

Tel: 617-354-7722

www.internationalist.com

PN@internationalist.com

Copyright © 2013 by PWN

The Internationalist is a Registered Trademark. "Key Facts" and "The Internationalist Business Guides" are Trademarks of The Internationalist Publishing Company.

All Rights are reserved under International, Pan-American, and Pan-Asian Conventions. No part of this book may be reproduced in any form without the written permission of the publisher. All rights vigorously enforced

Table Of Contents

Chapter 1: Background

Chapter 2: Geography

Chapter 3: People and Society

Chapter 4: Government and Key Leaders

Chapter 5: Economy

Chapter 6: Energy

Chapter 7: Communications

Chapter 8: Transportation

Chapter 9: Military

Chapter 10: Transnational Issues

Map of Bahrain

Chapter 1: Background

In 1783, the Sunni Al-Khalifa family captured Bahrain from the Persians. In order to secure these holdings, it entered into a series of treaties with the UK during the 19th century that made Bahrain a British protectorate. The archipelago attained its independence in 1971. Facing declining oil reserves, Bahrain has turned to petroleum processing and refining and has become an international banking center. Bahrain's small size and central location among Persian Gulf countries require it to play a delicate balancing act in foreign affairs among its larger neighbors. The Sunni-led government has struggled to manage relations with its large Shia-majority population. In early 2011, amid Arab uprisings elsewhere in the region, the Bahraini Government confronted similar protests at home with police and military action. The aftermath led to modest reforms, though continued dissatisfaction by Bahraini oppositionists with the extent of the reforms, has led to a broader dialogue between government officials, political societies, and legislators.

Chapter 2: Geography

Location:
　　Middle East, archipelago in the Persian Gulf, east of Saudi Arabia

Geographic coordinates:
　　26 00 N, 50 33 E

Map references:
　　Middle East

Area:
　　total: 760 sq km
　　country comparison to the world: 188
　　land: 760 sq km
　　water: 0 sq km

Area - comparative:
　　3.5 times the size of Washington, DC

Land boundaries:
　　0 km

Coastline:
　　161 km

Maritime claims:
　　territorial sea: 12 nm
　　contiguous zone: 24 nm
　　continental shelf: extending to boundaries to be determined

Climate:
　　arid; mild, pleasant winters; very hot, humid summers

Terrain:
　　mostly low desert plain rising gently to low central escarpment

Elevation extremes:
　　lowest point: Persian Gulf 0 m
　　highest point: Jabal ad Dukhan 122 m

Natural resources:

oil, associated and nonassociated natural gas, fish, pearls

Land use:

arable land: 1.79%

permanent crops: 3.95%

other: 94.26% (2011)

Irrigated land:

40.15 sq km (2003)

Total renewable water resources:

0.12 cu km (2011)

Freshwater withdrawal (domestic/industrial/agricultural):

total: 0.36 cu km/yr (50%/6%/45%)

per capita: 386 cu m/yr (2003)

Natural hazards:

periodic droughts; dust storms

Environment - current issues:

desertification resulting from the degradation of limited arable land, periods of drought, and dust storms; coastal degradation (damage to coastlines, coral reefs, and sea vegetation) resulting from oil spills and other discharges from large tankers, oil refineries, and distribution stations; lack of freshwater resources (groundwater and seawater are the only sources for all water needs)

Environment - international agreements:

party to: Biodiversity, Climate Change, Climate Change-Kyoto Protocol, Desertification, Hazardous Wastes, Law of the Sea, Ozone Layer Protection, Wetlands

signed, but not ratified: none of the selected agreements

Geography - note:

close to primary Middle Eastern petroleum sources; strategic location in Persian Gulf, through which much of the Western world's petroleum must transit to reach open ocean

Chapter 3: People and Society

Nationality:
>noun: Bahraini(s)
>adjective: Bahraini

Ethnic groups:
>Bahraini 46%, non-Bahraini 54% (2010 census)

Languages:
>Arabic (official), English, Farsi, Urdu

Religions:
>Muslim (Shia and Sunni) 81.2%, Christian 9%, other 9.8% (2001 census)

Population:
>1,281,332 July 2013 est.
>country comparison to the world: 156
>note: includes 235,108 non-nationals

Age structure:
>0-14 years: 20% (male 130,097/female 126,067)
>15-24 years: 15.9% (male 113,973/female 89,602)
>25-54 years: 56.2% (male 472,537/female 247,873)
>55-64 years: 5.2% (male 43,884/female 23,352)
>65 years and over: 2.6% (male 16,262/female 17,685) (2013 est.)

Median age:
>total: 31.4 years
>male: 32.8 years
>female: 28.6 years (2013 est.)

Population growth rate:
>2.57% (2013 est.)
>country comparison to the world: 25

Birth rate:
>14.16 births/1,000 population (2013 est.)
>country comparison to the world: 140

Death rate:

    2.65 deaths/1,000 population (2013 est.)

    country comparison to the world: 221

Net migration rate:

    14.13 migrant(s)/1,000 population (2013 est.)

    country comparison to the world: 9

Urbanization:

    urban population: 88.7% of total population (2011)

    rate of urbanization: 2.21% annual rate of change (2010-15 est.)

Major urban areas - population:

    MANAMA (capital) 262,000 (2011)

Sex ratio:

    at birth: 1.03 male(s)/female

    0-14 years: 1.03 male(s)/female

    15-24 years: 1.26 male(s)/female

    25-54 years: 1.92 male(s)/female

    55-64 years: 1.89 male(s)/female

    65 years and over: 0.91 male(s)/female

    total population: 1.54 male(s)/female (2013 est.)

Maternal mortality rate:

    20 deaths/100,000 live births (2010)

    country comparison to the world: 139

Infant mortality rate:

    total: 9.93 deaths/1,000 live births

    country comparison to the world: 144

    male: 11.1 deaths/1,000 live births

    female: 8.72 deaths/1,000 live births (2013 est.)

Life expectancy at birth:

    total population: 78.43 years

    country comparison to the world: 52

    male: 76.28 years

female: 80.63 years (2013 est.)

Total fertility rate:

1.83 children born/woman (2013 est.)

country comparison to the world: 152

Contraceptive prevalence rate:

61.8% (1995)

Health expenditures:

5% of GDP (2010)

country comparison to the world: 142

Physicians density:

1.44 physicians/1,000 population (2008)

Hospital bed density:

1.8 beds/1,000 population (2009)

Drinking water source:

improved:

urban: 100% of population (2010 est.)

Sanitation facility access:

improved:

urban: 100% of population (2010 est.)

HIV/AIDS - adult prevalence rate:

0.2% (2001 est.)

country comparison to the world: 103

HIV/AIDS - people living with HIV/AIDS:

fewer than 600 (2007 est.)

country comparison to the world: 148

HIV/AIDS - deaths:

fewer than 200 (2003 est.)

country comparison to the world: 106

Obesity - adult prevalence rate:

32.9% (2008)

country comparison to the world: 20

Education expenditures:
>2.9% of GDP (2008)
>
>country comparison to the world: 142

Literacy:
>definition: age 15 and over can read and write
>
>total population: 94.6%
>
>male: 96.1%
>
>female: 91.6% (2010 census)

School life expectancy (primary to tertiary education):
>total: 14 years
>
>male: 14 years
>
>female: 15 years (2006)

Child labor - children ages 5-14:
>total number: 5,530
>
>percentage: 5 % (2000 est.)

Unemployment, youth ages 15-24:
>total: 28.3%
>
>country comparison to the world: 31
>
>male: 25.7%
>
>female: 32.6% (2004)

Chapter 4: Government and Key Leaders

Country name:
> conventional long form: Kingdom of Bahrain
> conventional short form: Bahrain
> local long form: Mamlakat al Bahrayn
> local short form: Al Bahrayn
> former: Dilmun, State of Bahrain

Government type:
> constitutional monarchy

Capital:
> name: Manama
> geographic coordinates: 26 14 N, 50 34 E
> time difference: UTC+3 (8 hours ahead of Washington, DC during Standard Time)

Administrative divisions:
> 5 governorates (muhafazat, singular - muhafazah); Asamah (Capital), Janubiyah (Southern), Muharraq, Shamaliyah (Northern), Wasat (Central)
> note: each governorate administered by an appointed governor

Independence:
> 15 August 1971 (from the UK)

National holiday:
> National Day, 16 December (1971); note - 15 August 1971 was the date of independence from the UK, 16 December 1971 was the date of independence from British protection

Constitution:
> adopted 14 February 2002

Legal system:
> mixed legal system of Islamic law, English common law, Egyptian civil, criminal, and commercial codes; customary law

International law organization participation:
> has not submitted an ICJ jurisdiction declaration; non-party state to the ICCt

Suffrage:

20 years of age; universal; note - Bahraini Cabinet in May 2011 endorsed a draft law lowering eligibility to 18 years

Executive branch:

chief of state: King HAMAD bin Isa Al-Khalifa (since 6 March 1999); Crown Prince SALMAN bin Hamad Al-Khalifa (son of the monarch, born 21 October 1969)

head of government: Prime Minister KHALIFA bin Salman Al-Khalifa (since 1971); First Deputy Prime Minister SALMAN bin Hamad Al Khalifa (since 11 March 2013); Deputy Prime Ministers ALI bin Khalifa bin Salman Al-Khalifa, Jawad bin Salim al-ARAIDH, KHALID bin Abdallah Al Khalifa, MUHAMMAD bin Mubarak Al-Khalifa

cabinet: Cabinet appointed by the monarch

elections: the monarchy is hereditary; prime minister appointed by the monarch

Legislative branch:

bicameral National Assembly consists of the Shura Council or Consultative Council (40 members appointed by the King) and the Council of Representatives or Chamber of Deputies (40 seats; members directly elected to serve four-year terms)

elections: Council of Representatives - last held in two rounds on 23 and 30 October 2010 (next election to be held in 2014); byelections to fill 18 vacated seats held in two rounds on 24 September and 1 October 2011

election results: Council of Representatives (2010) - percent of vote by society - NA; seats by society - Wifaq (Shia) 18, Asalah (Sunni Salafi) 3, Minbar (Sunni Muslim Brotherhood) 2, independents 17; Council of Representatives byelection for 18 seats vacated by Wifaq (2011) - seats by society - independent Sunni 8, independent Shia 8, other 2; note - Bahrain has societies rather than parties

Judicial branch:

highest court(s): Court of Cassation (consists of a chairman and 3 judges); Constitutional Court (consists of a president and 6 members)

note - the judiciary of Bahrain is divided into the civil law and sharia law courts

judge selection and term of office: Court of Cassation and Constitutional Court judges appointed by royal decree and serve for a specified tenure

subordinate courts: High Court of Appeal; middle and lower civil courts; higher and lower shariah courts, and the High Shariah Court of Appeal

Political parties and leaders:
> note: political parties are prohibited but political societies were legalized per a July 2005 law
>
> progovernment:
>> Arab Islamic Center Society [Ahmad Sanad AL-BENALI]
>> Constitutional Gathering Society
>> Islamic Asalah [Abd al-Halim MURAD]
>> Islamic Saff Society [Abdullah Khalil BU GHAMAR]
>> Islamic Shura Society
>> Movement of National Justice Society [Muhi al-Din KHAN]
>> National Action Charter Society [Muhammad AL-BUAYNAYN]
>> National Dialogue Society
>> National Islamic Minbar [Ali AHMAD]
>> National Unity Gathering [Abdullah AL-HUWAYHI]
>
> oppositon:
>> National Democratic Action Society [Ibrahim SHARIF]
>> National Democratic Assembly [Hasan AL-ALI]
>> National Fraternity Society [Musa AL-ANSARI]
>> National Progressive Tribune [Abd al-Nabi SALMAN]
>> Unitary National Democratic Assemblage [Fadhil ABBAS]
>> Wifaq National Islamic Society [Ali SALMAN]

Political pressure groups and leaders:
> Sunni:
>> Al-Fatih Awakening
>
> Shia:
>> 14 February Revolution Youth Coalition
>> Bahrain Islamic Freedom Movement [Said SHIHABI]
>> Haqq Movement [Hasan MUSHAYMA]
>> Islamic Amal [Muhammad Ali AL-MAHFUDH]
>> Khalas [Abd al-Rauf AL-SHAYIB]
>> Wafa Islamic Society [Abd al-Wahab HUSAYN]

International organization participation:

ABEDA, AFESD, AMF, CAEU, CICA, FAO, G-77, GCC, IAEA, IBRD, ICAO, ICC (national committees), ICRM, IDA, IDB, IFC, IFRCS, IHO, ILO, IMF, IMO, IMSO, Interpol, IOC, IOM (observer), IPU, ISO, ITSO, ITU, ITUC (NGOs), LAS, MIGA, NAM, OAPEC, OIC, OPCW, PCA, UN, UNCTAD, UNESCO, UNIDO, UNWTO, UPU, WCO, WFTU (NGOs), WHO, WIPO, WMO, WTO

Diplomatic representation in the US:

chief of mission: Ambassador Huda Azra Ibrahim NUNU

chancery: 3502 International Drive NW, Washington, DC 20008

telephone: [1] (202) 342-1111

FAX: [1] (202) 362-2192

consulate(s) general: New York

Diplomatic representation from the US:

chief of mission: Ambassador Thomas C. KRAJESKI

embassy: Building #979, Road 3119 (next to Al-Ahli Sports Club), Block 331, Zinj District, Manama

mailing address: PSC 451, Box 660, FPO AE 09834-5100; international mail: American Embassy, Box 26431, Manama

telephone: [973] 1724-2700

FAX: [973] 1727-0547

Key Leaders:

King	HAMAD bin Isa Al Khalifa
Prime Min.	KHALIFA bin Salman Al Khalifa
First Dep. Prime Min.	SALMAN Bin Hamad Al Khalifa
Dep. Prime Min.	ALI bin Khalifa bin Salman Al Khalifa
Dep. Prime Min.	Jawad bin Salim al-ARAIDH
Dep. Prime Min.	KHALID bin Abdallah Al Khalifa
Dep. Prime Min.	MUHAMMAD bin Mubarak Al

	Khalifa
Min. of Culture	MAI bint Muhammad Al Khalifa
Min. of Education	Majid bin Ali Hasan al-NUAYMI
Min. of Energy	Abd al-Husayn MIRZA
Min. of Finance	AHMAD bin Muhammad bin Hamad bin Abdallah Al Khalifa
Min. of Foreign Affairs	KHALID bin Ahmad bin Muhammad Al Khalifa
Min. of Health	Sadiq bin Abd al-Karim al-SHIHABI
Min. of Housing	Basim bin Yacub al-HAMAR
Min. of Human Rights & Social Development	Fatima bint Ahmad al-BALUSHI
Min. of Industry & Commerce	HASAN bin Abdallah Fakhru
Min. of Interior	RASHID bin Abdallah bin Ahmad Al Khalifa
Min. of Justice & Islamic Affairs	KHALID bin Ali Al Khalifa
Min. of Labor	Jamil Muhammad Ali HUMAYDAN
Min. of Municipal Affairs & Urban Planning	JUMA bin Ahmad al-Ka'abi
Min. of the Royal Court	KHALID bin Ahmad bin Salman Al Khalifa

Min. of the Royal Court for Follow-Up Affairs	AHMAD BIN ATIYATALLAH Al Khalifa
Min. of Royal Court Affairs	ALI bin Isa bin Salman Al Khalifa
Min. of Transportation	KAMAL bin Ahmad Muhammad
Min. of Works	ISSAM bin Abdallah Khalaf
Min. of State for Defense Affairs	MUHAMMAD bin Abdallah Al Khalifa
Min. of State for Follow-Up Affairs	Muhammad bin Ibrahim al-MUTAWA
Min. of State for Foreign Affairs	Ghanim bin Fadhil al-BUAYNAYN
Min. of State for Human Rights Affairs	Salah ALI, *Dr.*
Min. of State for Information Affairs	Samira RAJAB
Min. of State for Interior Affairs	Adil Khalifa Hamad al-FADHIL
Min. of State for Shura Council & Parliament Affairs	Abd al-Aziz bin Muhammad al-FADHIL
Attorney Gen.	ALI bin Fadhil al-Buaynayn

Governor, Central Bank of Bahrain	Rashid bin Muhammad al-MARAJ
Ambassador to the US	Huda Azra Ibrahim NUNU
Permanent Representative to the UN, New York	Jamal Faris al-RUWAYI

Flag description:

red, the traditional color for flags of Persian Gulf states, with a white serrated band (five white points) on the hoist side; the five points represent the five pillars of Islam

note: until 2002 the flag had eight white points, but this was reduced to five to avoid confusion with the Qatari flag

National anthem:

name: "Bahrainona" (Our Bahrain)

lyrics/music: unknown

note: adopted 1971; although Mohamed Sudqi AYYASH wrote the original lyrics, they were changed in 2002 following the transformation of Bahrain from an emirate to a kingdom

Chapter 5: Economy

Economy - overview:

    Bahrain has taken great strides in diversifying its economy and its highly developed communication and transport facilities make Bahrain home to numerous multinational firms with business in the Gulf. As part of its diversification plans, Bahrain implemented a Free Trade Agreement (FTA) with the US in August 2006, the first FTA between the US and a Gulf state. Bahrain's economy, however, continues to depend heavily on oil. Petroleum production and refining account for more than 60% of Bahrain's export receipts, 70% of government revenues, and 11% of GDP. Other major economic activities are production of aluminum - Bahrain's second biggest export after oil - finance, and construction. Bahrain competes with Malaysia as a worldwide center for Islamic banking and continues to seek new natural gas supplies as feedstock to support its expanding petrochemical and aluminum industries. In 2011 and 2012, Bahrain experienced economic setbacks as a result of domestic unrest, however, several factors indicate that the economy is beginning to recover, such as the return of the formula one race and tourist cruise ships to Bahrain. Economic policies aimed at restoring confidence in Bahrain's economy, such as the suspension of an expatriate labor tax and frequent bailouts of Gulf Air, will make Bahrain's foremost long-term economic challenges - youth unemployment and the growth of government debt - more difficult to address.

GDP (purchasing power parity):

    $33.63 billion (2012 est.)

    country comparison to the world: 110

    $32.39 billion (2011 est.)

    $31.72 billion (2010 est.)

    note: data are in 2012 US dollars

GDP (official exchange rate):

    $27.03 billion (2012 est.)

GDP - real growth rate:

    3.9% (2012 est.)

    country comparison to the world: 85

2.1% (2011 est.)

4.7% (2010 est.)

GDP - per capita (PPP):

$29,200 (2012 est.)

country comparison to the world: 52

$28,700 (2011 est.)

$28,700 (2010 est.)

note: data are in 2012 US dollars

GDP - composition by sector:

agriculture: 0.4%

industry: 51.3%

services: 48.4% (2012 est.)

Labor force:

705,900

country comparison to the world: 150

note: 44% of the population in the 15-64 age group is non-national (2012 est.)

Labor force - by occupation:

agriculture: 1%

industry: 79%

services: 20% (1997 est.)

Unemployment rate:

15% (2005 est.)

country comparison to the world: 146

Population below poverty line:

NA%

Household income or consumption by percentage share:

lowest 10%: NA%

highest 10%: NA%

Investment (gross fixed):

20.4% of GDP (2012 est.)

country comparison to the world: 88

Budget:
    revenues: $8.378 billion
    expenditures: $8.675 billion (2012 est.)

Taxes and other revenues:
    31% of GDP (2012 est.)
    country comparison to the world: 88

Budget surplus (+) or deficit (-):
    -1.1% of GDP (2012 est.)
    country comparison to the world: 61

Public debt:
    54.3% of GDP (2012 est.)
    country comparison to the world: 53
    47.8% of GDP (2011 est.)

Inflation rate (consumer prices):
    2.8% (2012 est.)
    country comparison to the world: 85
    -0.4% (2011 est.)

Commercial bank prime lending rate:
    6.3% (31 December 2012 est.)
    country comparison to the world: 129
    6.83% (31 December 2011 est.)

Stock of narrow money:
    $7.777 billion (31 December 2012 est.)
    country comparison to the world: 84
    $7.013 billion (31 December 2011 est.)

Stock of broad money:
    $24.38 billion (31 December 2012 est.)
    country comparison to the world: 81
    $21.64 billion (31 December 2011 est.)

Stock of domestic credit:
    $24.31 billion (31 December 2012 est.)

country comparison to the world: 74

$20.78 billion (31 December 2011 est.)

Market value of publicly traded shares:

$17.15 billion (31 December 2011)

country comparison to the world: 63

$20.43 billion (31 December 2010)

$16.93 billion (31 December 2009)

Agriculture - products:

fruit, vegetables; poultry, dairy products; shrimp, fish

Industries:

petroleum processing and refining, aluminum smelting, iron pelletization, fertilizers, Islamic and offshore banking, insurance, ship repairing, tourism

Industrial production growth rate:

1.8% (2012 est.)

country comparison to the world: 103

Current account balance:

$2.846 billion (2012 est.)

country comparison to the world: 35

$3.247 billion (2011 est.)

Exports:

$21.4 billion (2012 est.)

country comparison to the world: 74

$19.91 billion (2011 est.)

Exports - commodities:

petroleum and petroleum products, aluminum, textiles

Exports - partners:

Saudi Arabia 3%, India 2.2%, UAE 2%, South Korea 1.9% (2012)

Imports:

$15.17 billion (2012 est.)

country comparison to the world: 88

$12.11 billion (2011 est.)

Imports - commodities:
> crude oil, machinery, chemicals

Imports - partners:
> Saudi Arabia 26.8%, US 9.7%, China 9.6%, Japan 6.4%, India 4.9%, France 4.7% (2012)

Reserves of foreign exchange and gold:
> $4.853 billion (31 December 2012 est.)
>
> country comparison to the world: 93
>
> $4.245 billion (31 December 2011 est.)

Debt - external:
> $27.12 billion (31 December 2012 est.)
>
> country comparison to the world: 75
>
> $27.04 billion (31 December 2011 est.)

Stock of direct foreign investment - at home:
> $16.87 billion (31 December 2012 est.)
>
> country comparison to the world: 75
>
> $15.94 billion (31 December 2011 est.)

Stock of direct foreign investment - abroad:
> $10.02 billion (31 December 2012 est.)
>
> country comparison to the world: 54
>
> $8.777 billion (31 December 2011 est.)

Exchange rates:
> Bahraini dinars (BHD) per US dollar:
>> 0.376 (2012 est.)
>>
>> 0.376 (2011 est.)
>>
>> 0.376 (2010 est.)
>>
>> 0.376 (2009)
>>
>> 0.376 (2008)

Fiscal year:
> calendar year

Chapter 6: Energy

Electricity - production:
>13.16 billion kWh (2011 est.)
>
>country comparison to the world: 87

Electricity - consumption:
>12.97 billion kWh (2011 est.)
>
>country comparison to the world: 81

Electricity - exports:
>0 kWh (2011 est.)
>
>country comparison to the world: 159

Electricity - imports:
>214 million kWh (2011 est.)
>
>country comparison to the world: 87

Electricity - installed generating capacity:
>3.168 million kW (2009 est.)
>
>country comparison to the world: 86

Electricity - from fossil fuels:
>100% of total installed capacity (2011 est.)
>
>country comparison to the world: 4

Electricity - from nuclear fuels:
>0% of total installed capacity (2011 est.)
>
>country comparison to the world: 44

Electricity - from hydroelectric plants:
>0% of total installed capacity (2011 est.)
>
>country comparison to the world: 156

Electricity - from other renewable sources:
>0% of total installed capacity (2011 est.)
>
>country comparison to the world: 107

Crude oil - production:
>44,800 bbl/day (2012 est.)

country comparison to the world: 63

Crude oil - exports:

152,600 bbl/day (2012 est.)

country comparison to the world: 35

Crude oil - imports:

256,000 bbl/day (2011 est.)

country comparison to the world: 29

Crude oil - proved reserves:

107.2 million bbl (1 January 2013 est.)

country comparison to the world: 71

Refined petroleum products - production:

270,800 bbl/day (2012 est.)

country comparison to the world: 48

Refined petroleum products - consumption:

51,450 bbl/day (2012 est.)

country comparison to the world: 98

Refined petroleum products - exports:

226,000 bbl/day (2012 est.)

country comparison to the world: 29

Refined petroleum products - imports:

0 bbl/day (2012 est.)

country comparison to the world: 209

Natural gas - production:

12.58 billion cu m (2010 est.)

country comparison to the world: 38

Natural gas - consumption:

12.25 billion cu m (2010 est.)

country comparison to the world: 44

Natural gas - exports:

0 cu m (2010 est.)

country comparison to the world: 58

Natural gas - imports:

0 cu m (2010 est.)

country comparison to the world: 156

Natural gas - proved reserves:

92.03 billion cu m (1 January 2012 est.)

country comparison to the world: 58

Carbon dioxide emissions from consumption of energy:

30.69 million Mt (2010 est.)

country comparison to the world: 77

Chapter 7: Communications

Telephones - main lines in use:
>276,500 (2011)
>country comparison to the world: 122

Telephones - mobile cellular:
>1.694 million (2011)
>country comparison to the world: 146

Telephone system:
>general assessment: modern system
>domestic: modern fiber-optic integrated services; digital network with rapidly growing use of mobile-cellular telephones
>international: country code - 973; landing point for the Fiber-Optic Link Around the Globe (FLAG) submarine cable network that provides links to Asia, Middle East, Europe, and US; tropospheric scatter to Qatar and UAE; microwave radio relay to Saudi Arabia; satellite earth station - 1 (2007)

Broadcast media:
>state-run Bahrain Radio and Television Corporation (BRTC) operates 5 terrestrial TV networks and several radio stations; satellite TV systems provide access to international broadcasts; 1 private FM station directs broadcasts to Indian listeners; radio and TV broadcasts from countries in the region are available (2007)

Internet country code:
>.bh

Internet hosts:
>47,727 (2012)
>country comparison to the world: 97

Internet users:
>419,500 (2009)
>country comparison to the world: 122

Chapter 8: Transportation

Airports:

    4 (2012)

    country comparison to the world: 185

Airports - with paved runways:

    total: 4

    over 3,047 m: 3

    914 to 1,523 m: 1 (2012)

Heliports:

    1 (2012)

Pipelines:

    gas 20 km; oil 54 km (2013)

Roadways:

    total: 4,122 km

    country comparison to the world: 156

    paved: 3,392 km

    unpaved: 730 km (2010)

Merchant marine:

    total: 8

    country comparison to the world: 119

    by type: bulk carrier 2, container 4, petroleum tanker 2

    foreign-owned: 5 (Kuwait 5)

    registered in other countries: 5 (Honduras 5) (2010)

Ports and terminals:

    Mina' Salman, Sitrah

Chapter 9: Military

Military branches:

Bahrain Defense Force (BDF): Royal Bahraini Army (RBA), Royal Bahraini Navy (RBN), Royal Bahraini Air Force (RBAF), Royal Bahraini Air Defense Force (RBADF) (2013)

Military service age and obligation:

18 years of age for voluntary military service; 15 years of age for NCOs, technicians, and cadets; no conscription (2012)

Manpower available for military service:

males age 16-49: 508,863

females age 16-49: 290,801 (2010 est.)

Manpower fit for military service:

males age 16-49: 423,757

females age 16-49: 245,302 (2010 est.)

Manpower reaching militarily significant age annually:

male: 8,988

female: 8,117 (2010 est.)

Military expenditures:

4.5% of GDP (2006)

country comparison to the world: 20

Chapter 10: Transnational Issues

Disputes - international:
 none

Map of Bahrain

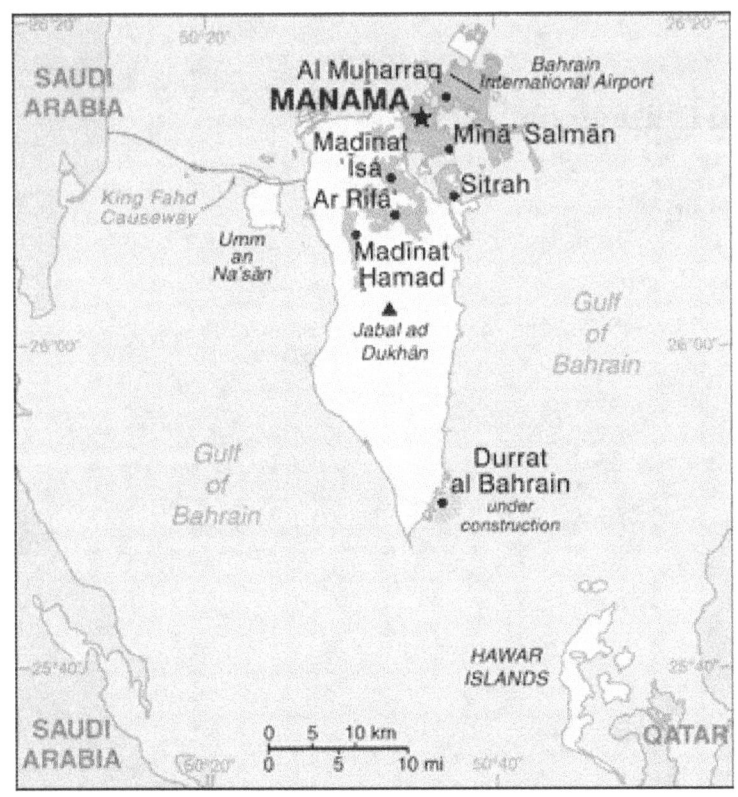

Other Key Facts™ Titles

Key Facts on Syria

Key Facts on China

Key Facts on Qatar

Key Facts on India

Key Facts on Germany

Key Facts on Argentina

Key Facts on Russia

Key Facts on North Korea

Key Facts on Brazil

Key Facts on Italy

Key Facts on the United Arab Emirates

Key Facts on the European Union

Key Facts on Pakistan

Key Facts on Saudi Arabia

Key Facts on Cyprus

Key Facts on Iran

Key Facts on Afghanistan

Key Facts on Iraq

Key Facts on Indonesia

Key Facts on South Korea

Key Facts on France

Key Facts on the United Kingdom

Key Facts on Egypt

Key Facts on Israel

Key Facts on Mexico

Key Facts on the United States of America

Key Facts on Turkey

Key Facts on South Africa

Key Facts on Greece

Key Facts on Japan

Key Facts on Malaysia

Key Facts on Vietnam

Key Facts on Hong Kong

Key Facts on Jordan

Key Facts on Australia

Key Facts on Venezuela

Key Facts on Canada

Key Facts on Burma (Myanmar)

Key Facts on Myanmar (Burma)

Key Facts on Singapore

Key Facts on Ireland

Key Facts on The Philippines

Key Facts on Thailand

Key Facts on Yemen

All Key Facts™ Titles are Available at www.Amazon.com

THE INTERNATIONALIST®
2013
WWW.INTERNATIONALIST.COM

www.ingramcontent.com/pod-product-compliance
Lightning Source LLC
Chambersburg PA
CBHW070728180526
45167CB00004B/1659